WHO LIVED IN PERU BEFORE THE INCA EMPIRE? THE EARLY TRIBES

History of the World

Children's History Books

BABY PROFESSOR

EDUCATION KIDS

The most famous civilization in Peru before the Europeans arrived was the Inca Empire. But there were many cultures in the area before the Inca! Let's find out about them!

THE MOST ANCIENT CITY IN THE AMERICAS

THE NORTE CHICO

The Norte Chico people flourished from around 3,000 to 1,700 BCE. They may have been the first city-dwellers in the Americas. They had more than thirty large cities, but evidence of this civilization only began coming to light in the 1990s.

The Norte Chico had complex irrigation systems to bring water to their fields and to their cities, and they built stepped pyramids (stepped pyramids look from the side like you could walk up them like a staircase, unlike the pyramids of Egypt which had smooth sides).

STEP PYRAMID

CARAL

This culture created intricate woven textiles, but they did not make pottery or ceramics. Their biggest city, Caral, had no defensive walls and may have been mainly a city for religious events.

As well as textiles, the Norte Chico may have invented an early writing system of the Americas, the quipu. A quipu message was "written" using patterns of knots in a series of threads, and the Inca Empire used it widely. It was still in use well into the nineteenth century in parts of Peru.

For some reason the Norte Chico culture ran into difficulties and its people abandoned its cities. We don't yet know what happened to this civilization.

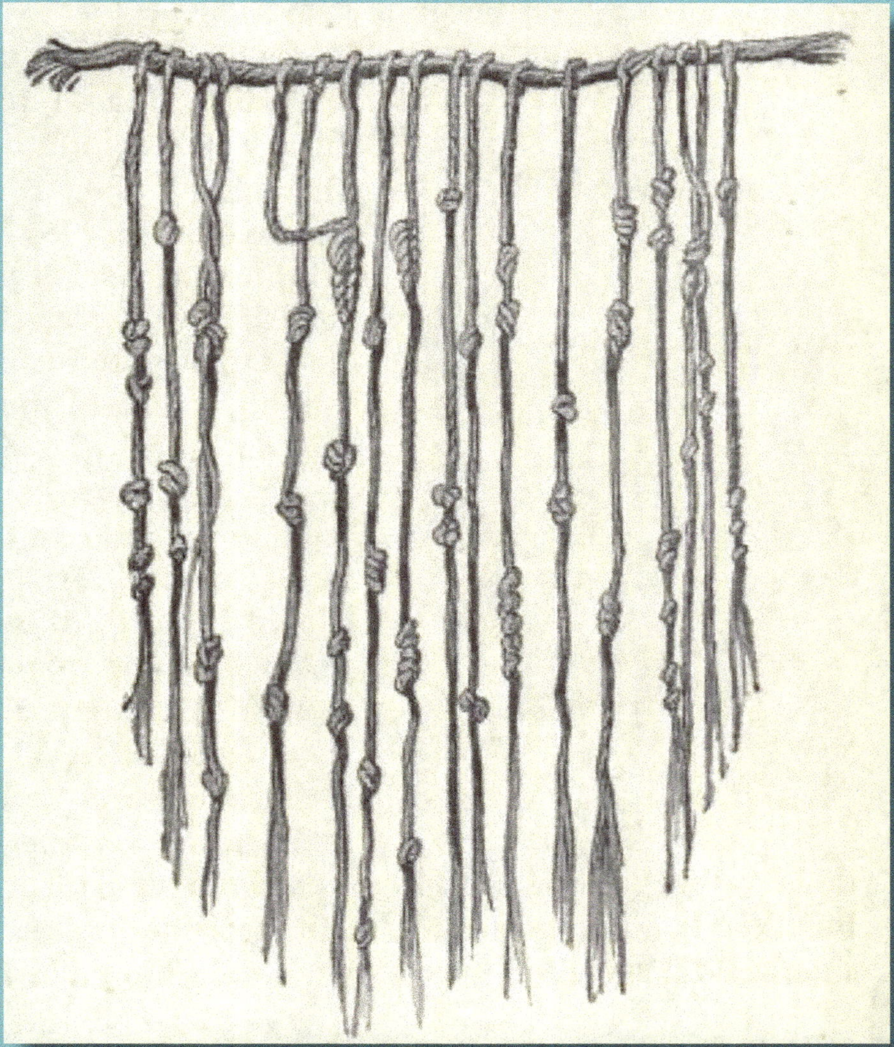

QUIPU

CHAVIN DE HUANTAR TEMPLE COMPLEX, ANCASH PROVINCE, PERU

THE CHAVIN

The Chavin culture emerged around 900 BCE, was at its most powerful around 500, and declined around 200 BCE. They lived in valleys in the west-central part of Peru, in cities that did not have defensive walls. There is no sign that they had wars with other cultures.

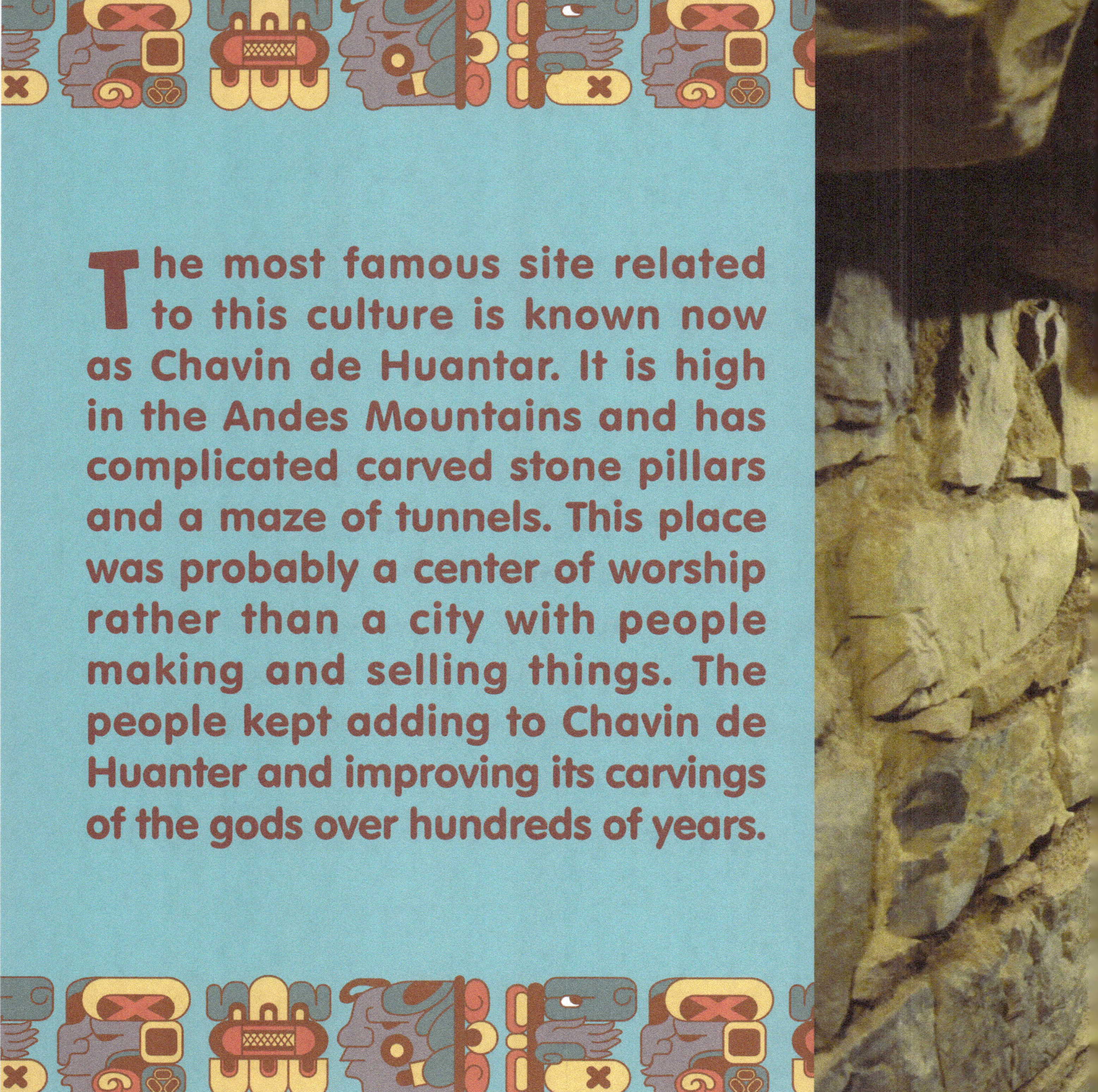

The most famous site related to this culture is known now as Chavin de Huantar. It is high in the Andes Mountains and has complicated carved stone pillars and a maze of tunnels. This place was probably a center of worship rather than a city with people making and selling things. The people kept adding to Chavin de Huanter and improving its carvings of the gods over hundreds of years.

UNDERGROUND TUNNELS WITHIN THE MAIN
TEMPLE OF CHAVIN DE HUANTAR, ANCASH, PERU

LANDSCAPE IN PARACAS NATIONAL PARK
RESERVE, PISCO, PERU

THE PARACAS

Most of the world's civilizations developed along river valleys. The Paracas, who flourished between 700 and 200 BCE, built their culture along Peru's coast . They had complicated irrigation systems for their crops, and made beautiful fabrics of woven cloth. They are many Paracas tombs, and mummies of the important people who were buried in them.

THE MOCHE

The Moche culture developed in northern Peru starting about 100 CE, and continued until about 800. It was more a combination of city-states, like ancient Greece, than a single nation. Their early cities were not fortified, but later cities show evidence of preparations for war.

ANCIENT PYRAMID KNOWN AS THE HUACA DEL SOL
IN TRUJILLO, PERU

The Moche build huge pyramids and created wonderful jewelry and other items from metal. They built a pyramid, the Huaca del Sol, that was probably the largest structure made by humans in the Americas before the arrival of the Europeans. The pyramid was made from more than 130 million bricks.

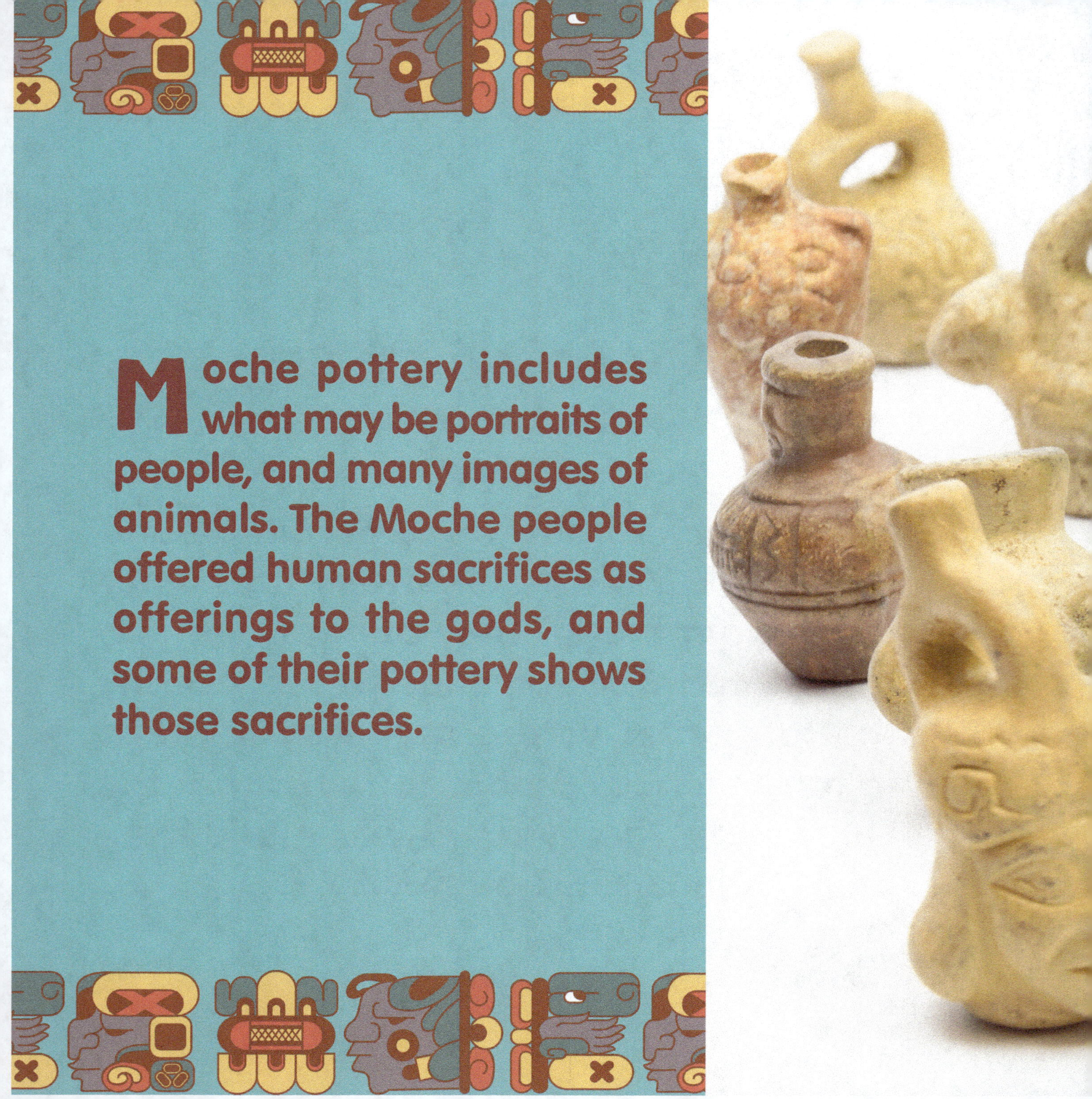

Moche pottery includes what may be portraits of people, and many images of animals. The Moche people offered human sacrifices as offerings to the gods, and some of their pottery shows those sacrifices.

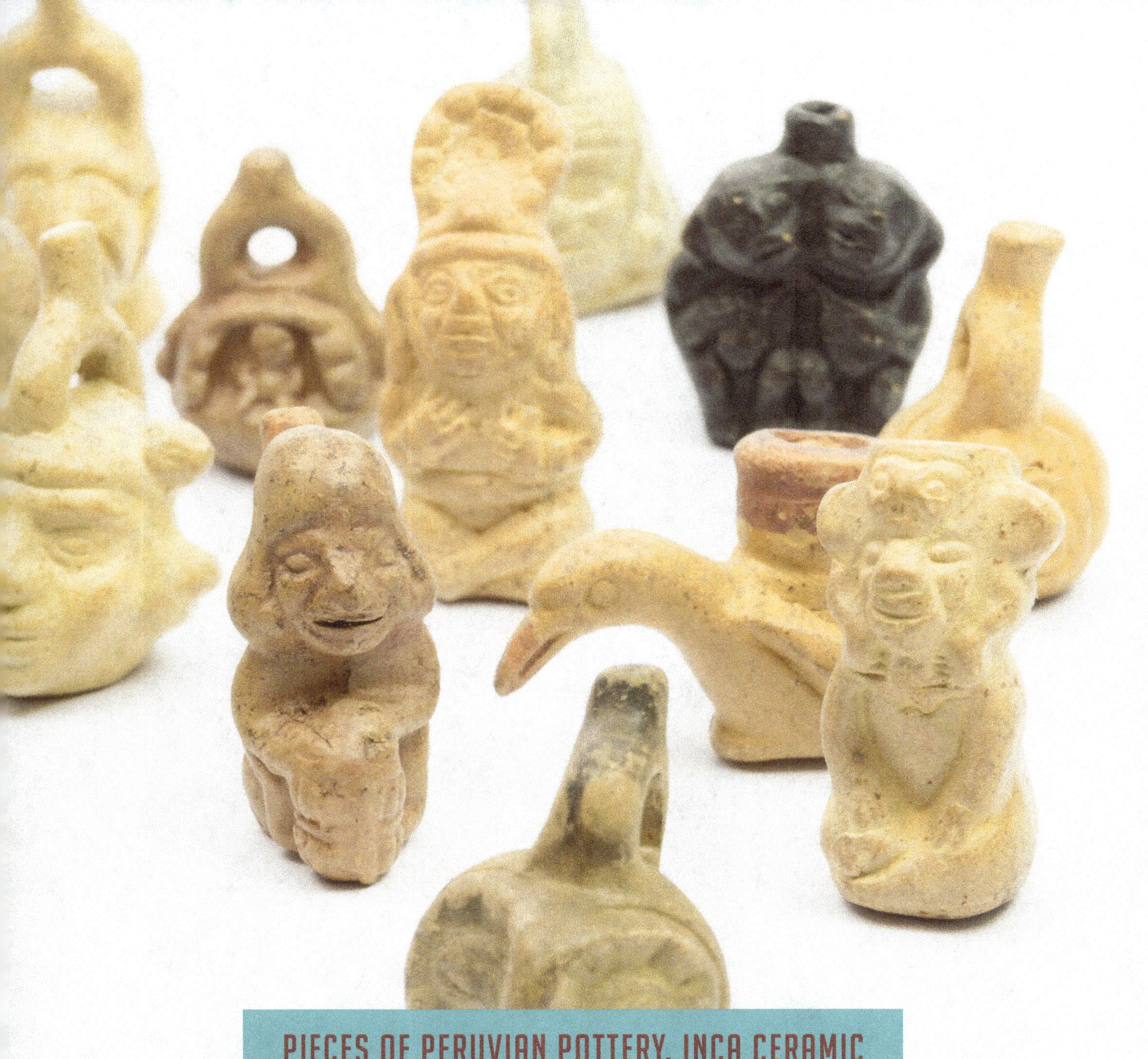

PIECES OF PERUVIAN POTTERY, INCA CERAMIC

ISLA
LOS
UROS
ISLA
LOS
UROS
PERUVIAN GOD TUMI SOUVENIRS

The sacred knife used in the sacrifice was called a "tumi", and this term persists in South America to describe physical objects that connect this world to the world of the gods.

It's possible a climate-change event, or a drought lasting many years, undermined this culture and caused it to collapse. Even human sacrifices could not bring enough rain!

DROUGHT CRACKED DESERT LANDSCAPE

GATE OF THE SUN AT TIWANAKU

THE TIWANACU

The Tiwanacu, or Tiahuanaco, developed their culture in southern Peru, near lake Titicaca, between 600 and 1100. Their central city had as many as 50,000 people living in it. They were excellent builders in stone, and created huge temple complexes. There is a stone arch called the Gateway of the Sun which is still standing.

Some people have argued that the central city, high up in the Andes Mountains, may be more than nine thousand years old, but most historians think it is much younger than that.

TIWANACU, OLD SCULPTURES

RICE TERRACE

THE HUARI

The Huari civilization was related to the Tiwanacu, and traded with them, but seem to have been a different culture. It reached its peak around 800 and then mysteriously collapsed about one hundred years later.

The Huari had a good system of roads and built terraces to grow crops up the sides of steep mountains (a terraced hillside has a series of flat fields, like steps, created by carving away a lot of the steep hillside over many years).

Their central government supported itself by collecting taxes on both farmers and merchants. One of their cities, Pikillacta, had at least 700 buildings made of stone, some of them more than three stories tall.

RUINS OF THE OLD INCA TOWN OF PIKILLACTA

NAZCA DESERT IN PERU, SOUTH AMERICA

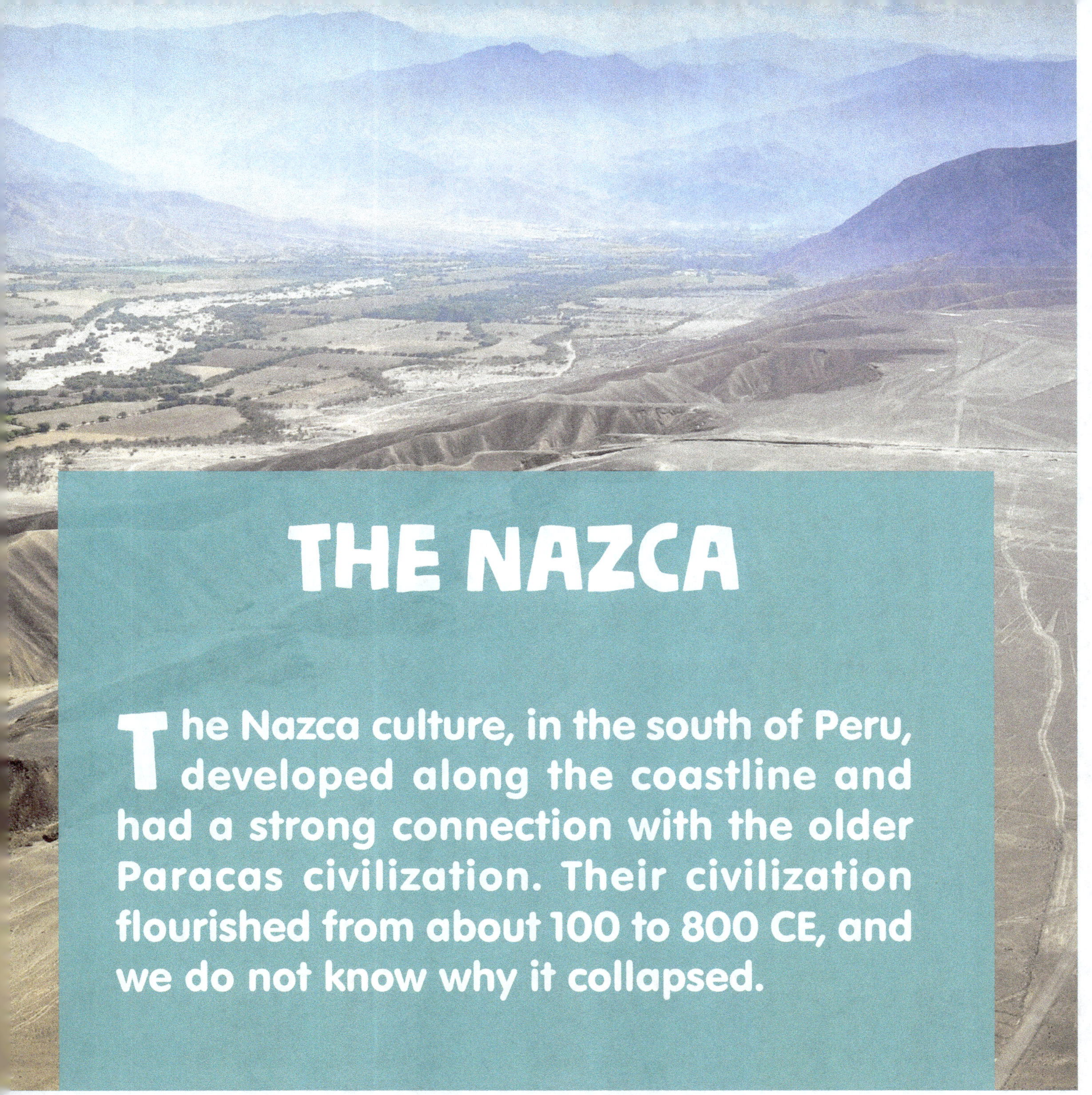

THE NAZCA

The Nazca culture, in the south of Peru, developed along the coastline and had a strong connection with the older Paracas civilization. Their civilization flourished from about 100 to 800 CE, and we do not know why it collapsed.

They lived in a very dry area and had to be inventive to get enough water to their crops. They either built underground water channels, or used channels that the Paracas people before them had built. The Nazca had central worship centers, with pyramids, but they left behind few physical items to study.

NAZCA PYRAMID

NAZCA LINES, AERIAL VIEW, PERU, THE HUMMINGBIRD

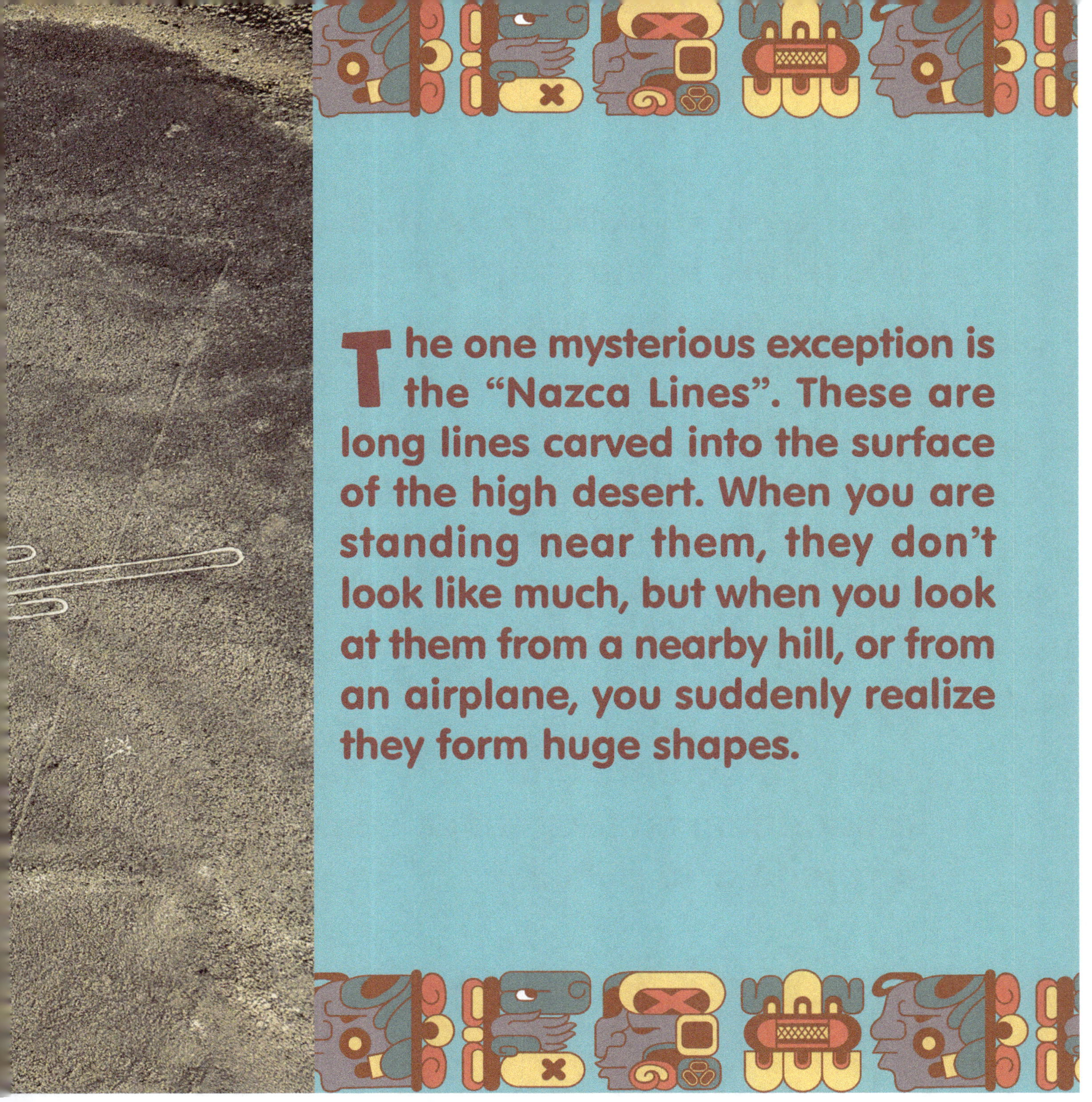

The one mysterious exception is the "Nazca Lines". These are long lines carved into the surface of the high desert. When you are standing near them, they don't look like much, but when you look at them from a nearby hill, or from an airplane, you suddenly realize they form huge shapes.

Nobody knows why the Nazca put in the effort to make these shapes. Some people say they might be landing strips for visitors from outer space! In some areas, along with the sets of straight lines, there are huge carved images of birds, monkeys, llamas, trees, and even fish. Some of the lines and figures are more than six hundred feet long.

Since you can't make out the images when you are close to them, it is hard even to understand how the creators made them so they make sense from an airplane or a hillside!

Nazca
Lines

NAZCA LINES TRAPEZIUM GEOGLYPHS IN PERU

Here are some interesting facts about the Nazca Lines:

- There are more than 800 straight lines, more than seventy images of animals and plants, and more than 300 squares, triangles, and other symbols.

- There don't seem to be any mistakes, where the makers had to fill in lines and try again! They got it right the first time, each time.

- To make the lines, the creators carefully removed the surface layer of the desert, which is made up of small reddish stones. This leaves the lines in a contrasting color of grayish clay.

- The lines are very shallow. They have lasted so long because the high Peruvian desert is extremely dry. It sees almost no rainfall, so there is no water to wash away or erode the designs, and no plant life to grow over them.

NAZCA LINES DRAWN ON STONES WHICH ARE BEING SOLD
TO TOURISTS AS SOUVENIRS FROM PERU

NAZCA LINES SPIRAL GEOGLYPH IN PERU

- Some people think you can only see the lines and designs from an airplane—or a space ship! But most of them are visible from the hills nearby.

- The longest series of images and lines covers about nine miles.

- **Some scientists think that the Nazca were working out mathematical principles, or calculations related to the stars. The "spider" design may be related to the position of the stars that make up the constellation Orion.**

CONSTELLATION ORION

AERIAL VIEW OF FARMS AND DESERT AROUND NAZCA, PERU

○ Other scientists think the patterns and images may have been related to religious worship and rituals, and that it was a way of asking for favors from the gods. The key request might have been for water to let the forests grow so there would be a lot of fruit and animals.

The Nazca and Moche cultures collapsed about the same time, and some historians suggest there may have been some climate-change event that forced the people to leave their cities and move to other areas. It is also possible that they may have been conquered, or worn out by a long series of wars for which we now have no record.

THE CHIMU

The Chimu culture followed the Moche in northern Peru, developing around 900. The ruins of the huge Chimu capital, Chan Chan, can still be visited. It covered more than ten square miles.

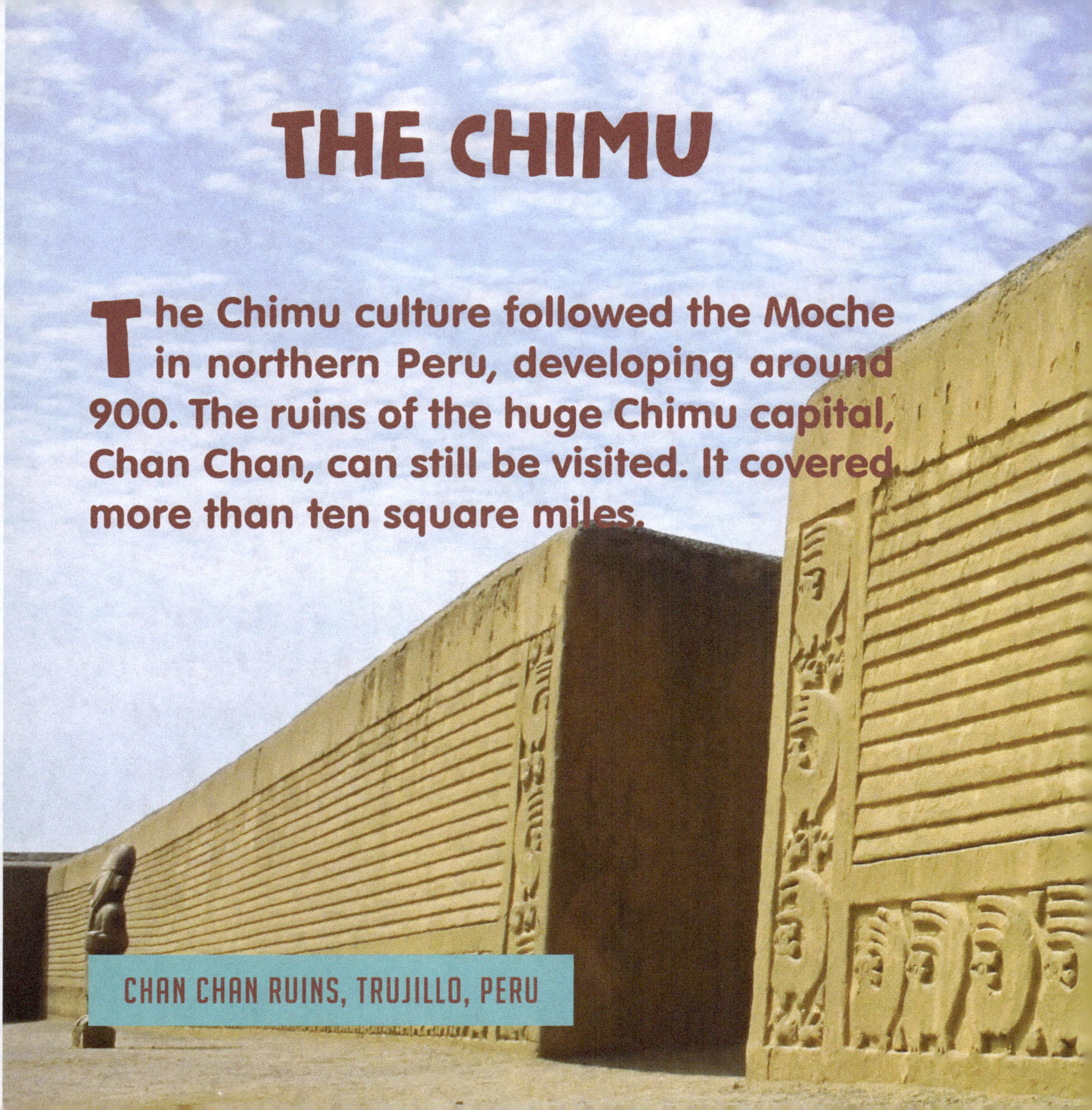

CHAN CHAN RUINS, TRUJILLO, PERU

IRRIGATION SYSTEM WATERING PLANTS

The culture developed along the fertile coastal strip of Peru, which is very narrow. They were well-organized and were good at warfare. Their success at growing crops meant they could support a large army.

Around 1300 the Chimu started expanding, absorbing other peoples until its territory covered most of central and northern Peru. This put them into conflict with another rising state, the Inca Empire. When the two empires collided, the Chimu were conquered and absorbed.

MACHU PICCHU, MAIN TEMPLE OF INCA EMPIRE.

WHAT HAPPENED NEXT?

All of the people and territories came together and became part of the Inca Empire. Learn about it in Baby Professor books like The History of the Inca Empire, Inca Government and Society, and The Two Major Cities of the Inca Empire: Cuzco and Machu Picchu.

Visit

BABY PROFESSOR
EDUCATION KIDS

www.BabyProfessorBooks.com

to download Free Baby Professor eBooks
and view our catalog of new and exciting
Children's Books

www.ingramcontent.com/pod-product-compliance
Lightning Source LLC
Chambersburg PA
CBHW080803180726
48003CB00022BA/2944